FINNISH
FOLKTALES

Timeless Stories fromFinland

A.S. MASON

Disclaimer

The author is solely responsible for this book's information, ideas, and opinions; they do not necessarily represent the views of any institutions, organizations, or individuals associated with the author. The author has made what they believe to be reasonable steps to make sure that the material contained in this book is accurate. However, neither the author nor the publisher makes any representations or guarantees, either stated or implied, regarding the completeness, accuracy, reliability, appropriateness, or availability of the content contained within. It is strongly recommended that readers seek assistance from relevant professionals or specialists in specific disciplines by consulting with them to acquire precise information tailored to their particular situations. The author disclaims liability for any loss, damage, or harm resulting from using the information provided in this book and any omissions or errors.

This book may reference websites, goods, services, or resources owned or operated by third parties. These references are solely offered for your convenience, and their inclusion does not indicate that we approve, sponsor, or recommend the content provided by the third party. Because the author and the publisher do not have any control over the nature, content, or availability of external websites, they cannot be held liable for any actions, decisions, or consequences resulting from using such external resources.

This book is for you,

The dreamers who wander through the enchanted forests of ancient lore, the seekers who dive into the depths of oceans where gods, goddesses and monsters dwell, and the storytellers who breathe life into the legends of old.

Thank you for keeping the magic alive.

About the Author

A.S. Mason is a passionate mythologist and historian who brings a unique blend of academic rigour and storytelling flair to the exploration of world mythologies. This early interest grew into a lifelong quest to learn how different cultures use myths to explain the world and pass on their beliefs. They have done studies in places like the sun-baked ruins of Mesopotamia and the misty temples of Japan, always looking for the common themes that run through different mythologies.

Readers are taken on a full and interesting journey through the myths that have shaped society. Mason uses careful study, interesting stories, and deep analysis to get people to think about the myths' lasting power and how they still apply today.

TABLE OF CONTENTS

INTRODUCTION

Finnish folklore has been interesting to people for a very long time. It is full of tales, memories, and stories. These stories come from the beliefs of the Finnish people. However, they have changed over time because of things that happened in history, cultural exchanges, and the unique surroundings of Finland. In the past, the ancestors of modern Finns came to the area. This is where Finnish folklore began. Folklore in Finland is based on the ideas and stories that the first people who came to the country brought with them. Their stories began to show how closely people are linked to nature as they got used to living in the cold North. This is still a big part of Finnish mythology.

Over the years, many different cultures have mixed with Finnish myth and changed it. They were close to Scandinavian countries, so some of their stories were like Norse folklore. But talking to Baltic and Slavic people added new things to the old ones. Finnish folklore, on the other hand, stayed different. The main reason for this is that many Finnish towns were pretty far away from each other, and strong oral customs kept these stories alive.

Many parts of Finnish culture have been passed down from one generation to the next through rune singing, which is the act of singing myth-based stories. Runonlaulajat were people who sang runes. They passed on old information and were an important part of Finnish culture. Folk Finnish string instruments, called the kantele, were often played along with their songs, which helped people remember the stories.

People started to really study and record Finnish culture in the 1800s when Finland was becoming more independent. History buffs and researchers went all over Finland to record and gather the stories that people in the countryside had told each other over the years. Without this work, many stories would have been lost. It also changed the way Finns think about their country. A doctor and folklorist named Elias The Kalevala, Finland's national classic, was written by Lönnrot. He was very important to this project. Lönnrot's work, which came out in 1835 and was made better in 1849, put together a lot of different folk songs and stories into one story that told about Finnish folklore. After "The Kalevala" came out, there were changes in how Finnish culture was shared and kept living.

Finns' stories changed over time as the country

became more modern. As time went on and people learned to read and write, they heard and told these stories in different ways. People learned about many old beliefs in new ways or mixed them with Christian beliefs. This made a unique mix of old religious practices and new religious ideas. Finland's folk music is still a big part of the country's culture. A lot of myths and stories aren't the same as they used to be, but people still find their characters and ideas interesting. Folklore has affected many parts of modern Finnish culture, from writing and art to music and pop culture. It links the present to the past.

There is a big book called The Kalevala that has come to define Finnish culture. It is at the centre of Finnish tradition. Elias Lönnrot put together this epic poem in the 1800s. It's more than just a bunch of old stories. It's a big part of Finnish writing and makes the country proud. This poem has 50 parts called runos or cantos. Together, they make up about 23,000 lines. It combines many different folk songs and myths into one story that spans from the start of time to the time when Christianity came to Finland. The epic is about three main characters: Väinämöinen, who is old and wise; Ilmarinen, who is a skilled blacksmith; and Lemminkäinen, who is daring and likes to take risks.

In Finnish history, it was a very important year.

It was that time when Russia had Finland as a Grand Duchy, and people there were becoming more patriotic. The Kalevala helped Finns understand what made their society unique and connected them to a shared saga of the past. An important part of making Finland a country was this. There was a lot more to the Kalevala than just being creative. The epic shaped a wave of art and culture. It was named after the place where a lot of the epic's material came from. The Kalevala gave many ideas to artists, singers, and writers. They got ideas for their work from Finnish tales and folklore. An important singer named Jean Sibelius used ideas from the Kalevala in many of his pieces.

Many people around the world read and thought about the Kalevala. The Kalevala is still very important to Finns. On February 28, every year, people celebrate Kalevala Day. Kids read about it in the news and learn about it in school. People today might find the old language and stories hard to follow, but Finns still care a lot about the book's ideas and characters. Folklore and stories told by mouth can be very powerful, as shown in the Kalevala. It's important to share old stories, and they can also become national stories that bring everyone together. Because of this, learning about Finnish tradition and the culture that makes Finland what it is today is still very important.

There are many different kinds of gods, heroes, and supernatural beings in Finnish folklore. Each one represents a different part of nature, the human experience, or the universe. These characters and the ideas they stand for are at the heart of Finnish folklore. They show us what people in ancient Finland believed, feared, and hoped for. The main hero of the Kalevala, Väinämöinen, is one of the most important people in Finnish mythology. Väinämöinen stands for knowledge, creativity, and the power of song. He is often represented as an old, wise man who can do magic. His words and songs had the power to change the world. This shows how important art and learning are in Finland.

Ilmarinen, who is the eternal blacksmith, is another important person. Ilmarinen is famous for being a very skilled artist. He is said to have made the Sampo and the dome of the sky. The fact that he is skilled, works hard, and comes up with new ideas shows how much these traits are valued in Finnish society. The third main figure in the Kalevala, Lemminkäinen, has a different set of traits. Lemminkäinen is the perfect example of a young man who is full of energy and eager to find love. His trips to the otherworld and his mother's resurrections show how loyal people can be, how powerful motherly love can be, and how life and death repeat themselves.

In Finnish mythology, the women figures are just as important as the men. Louhi is the mistress of Pohjola (the North). She is a strong and often hostile character. Her character is like the harsh northern climate and the problems it brings. Her daughter, the Maiden of Pohjola, is a beautiful woman whom people want to marry. The Kalevala is mostly about her search for a husband. As a result of the close connection between the Finnish people and their surroundings, nature gods are very important in Finnish mythology. Ukko, the god of thunder, was one of the most important gods. He was linked to the crops, the weather, and fertility. Tapio was the forest god, and Mielikki was his wife. They were very important to hunting rites and forest stories.

The soul is also a big part of Finnish myth. The Finns of the past believed that people had more than one soul, like the luonto (nature essence) and the haltija (guardian spirit). This complex view of the soul shows a range of ideas about how we think and feel and how we are connected to nature. Animism, the idea that everything has a spirit or soul, is a big part of Finnish lore. This view of the world can be seen in the many nature spirits that appear in Finnish tales, such as the väki (elemental forces) and the haltija of certain places or things.

In Finnish folklore, too, the ideas of creation and the

order of the universe are explored. In Finnish origin stories, the world is said to have been made from the pieces of a big egg. This idea is called the "world egg." They often do things that older pagan gods used to do. Folklore changes over time, and it's hard to figure out what happened in Finland's holy past.

We can learn about how the old Finns saw the world by looking at their ideas and stories about people. It's not a very nice or painful place. Many stories are about trips to and from Tuonela that show themes of death, the future, and the thin line that separates the living and the dead. In Finnish mythology, magic and shamanism are prominent. With magical powers and the ability to travel between different worlds, the tietäjä (sage or shaman) figure shows how important spiritual knowledge is and how everything is linked. When Christianity came to Finland, it brought with it an interesting mix of old and new stories. There are times when Christians like Saint Peter or Jesus show up in folk tales. They often do things that older pagan gods used to do. Folklore changes over time, and it's hard to figure out what happened in Finland's holy past.

We can learn about how the old Finns saw the world by looking at their ideas and stories about people. In them, people live close to nature, value learning and skill, and know how fragile the balance is between the world's different forces. In these stories, we can see how the hopes, fears, and beliefs of the Finns shaped their society, and they still do. The strong bond between the Finnish people and their natural surroundings is one thing that makes Finnish tales stand out. People in old Finland thought that everything in nature had a spirit or mind. This is where the idea of this connection comes from.

Finns believed that forests, lakes, rocks, and even single trees had guardian spirits that lived there. These spirits were called haltijas. It wasn't like these ghosts were far away and unknown; you could talk to them, make them happy, or even make a deal with them. This set of beliefs made people deeply respect nature and changed how they dealt with their surroundings. Finnish myth has a lot to say about the forest in particular. Tapio was the forest god, and Mielikki was his wife. They were very important in hunting practices and forest stories. Before going into the bush, hunters would make offerings to these gods and ask for permission to do so. Not only did this show respect for nature, but it also showed that people knew they needed to keep the ecosystem in order.

People who live in water also have important roles in Finnish folktales. People thought that Ahti, the god of the deep, and Vellamo, the goddess of water, were in charge of the water and all the living things that lived in it. The fisherman gave these gods gifts to make sure they got a lot of fish and had a safe trip. People in Finland thought that the country's many lakes, rivers, and seas were entrances to other worlds. This made these sources of water mysterious and dangerous.

Another important part of Finnish animism is the idea of väki or natural forces. People thought that different nature events had their väki. For example, there was a fire-väki, a water-väki, a forest-väki, and so on. Some people who are good at magic could use these forces to heal, protect, or do other magical things. People who held this view believed that nature was not only alive but also had power that could be used and interacted with.

Seasonal changes were a big part of Finnish culture, which was based on the big changes that happened in the northern climate. A lot of the routines and traditions were connected to the seasons, from planting ceremonies in the spring to parties in the middle of winter. In Finland, the long, dark winters and short, hot summers left their mark on the stories and myths, which often made the seasonal changes into fights between light and dark.

Animals play a big role in Finnish folk tales. They are often shown to be smart, have their own cultures, and be able to change how they look. When people saw bears, they thought of them as holy animals with strong ties to people. People respected bears so much that they didn't use their real names. Instead, they used euphemisms like "honey-paw" or "forest apple."

The Finnish origin story, told in the Kalevala, is based on images from nature. Duck eggshell pieces make up the world. The moon is made of the white part, the sun is made of the yolk, and the stars are made of the shell bits. The idea behind this story of how the universe was made is that nature and the universe are connected in a way that can't be broken.

Animism in Finland is also based on the idea of luonto, which means "personal nature." People thought that each person had a luonto, which was a spirit or soul that was connected to nature. If your luonto was weak, it could make you sick or give you bad luck. If it was strong, it meant you were strong and skilled. People believe this because it shows how they connect the outdoor world to their health.

In Finnish shamanism, which had a lot to do with nature, the tietäjä, or teacher figure, was very important. Many people thought these people could go to other places, talk to plants and animals, or change into them. During their practices, they would often fall into trances by beating drums or singing. In their minds, the beats and sounds of nature were even stronger because of this.

In Finnish mythology, the supernatural view of the world includes things and places that people made. People believed that houses, tools, and even weapons had their spirits or haltijas. Because of this belief, people had different practices and customs for making and using things and for building and maintaining homes.

This can be seen in their environmental laws and in the common practice of spending time in nature for mental and physical health. So, nature and ancestry play more than just a telling part in Finnish folktales. It shows a complete view of the world that shaped how ancient Finns saw their place in the universe, dealt with their surroundings, and set up their society. This long history continues to teach us important lessons about how to live in harmony with nature and how people are deeply connected to it.

Ajatar: The Evil Spirit
Of The Forest

T here is a scary spirit called Ajatar who lives in the deep, dark woods of Finland. People who go too far into the woods are scared of this scary creature that has been a part of Finnish myth for hundreds of years. Ajatar isn't like most people who live in forests; she's a bad force that makes everyone who comes across her miserable.

Imagine a woman whose body is a snake and whose hair is a mess of snakes twisting together. This is how the Finns thought of Ajatar in the past. Some people said her eyes had a scary glow, and her breath smelled like death. As she moved through the woods, she brought sickness and gave up hope.

Ajatar wasn't just any forest spirit. People said she was the "devil of the woods" and caused sickness and death. There are old stories that say she could make people sick just by looking at them. When hunters and tourists got sick after going through the forest, they would often blame Ajatar. They thought she could spread her diseases through the air and infect anyone who breathed them in. Ajatar was bad in more ways than just making people sick, however. People also said she could confuse and disorient travellers and lead them wrong. People who got lost in the Finnish woods were thought to be under Ajatar's spell and would keep going in circles until they died of hunger, thirst, or the cold.

People were scared of Ajatar so much that they would leave her gifts at the forest's edge to try to calm her down and stay out of her way. As a way to ask for safety, these gifts are left in her area. They could be small animals or food. To understand Ajatar, we need to learn more about Finnish legends. Another fictional being like Ajatar didn't live by himself. Finns, in the past, believed she was part of a complex web of gods and spirits that controlled different parts of nature.

Ajatar's family tree goes back to Hiisi, a scary person in Finnish mythology. Hiisi was known as the "master of the woods," a strong and often evil spirit that lived in holy groves and rock formations. As Hiisi's daughter, Ajatar got his connection to the forest, but she played a more specific and evil part. Lempo is another scary figure in Finnish mythology that is related to Ajatar in some stories. People often say that Lempo is a monster or evil spirit that is linked to love and fertility in a bad way. Some stories say that Ajatar and Lempo were brothers and both born to Hiisi. Other stories say that they were lovers or even two different forms of the same evil force.

People also said that Ajatar was linked to the Gnomes in Finnish folklore. These were not the friendly yard gnomes we think of today. Instead, they were forest spirits who liked to get into trouble and were sometimes dangerous. People thought that the gnomes helped Ajatar do bad things by keeping an eye on her in the forest and telling her about possible victims.

Matthew lived in a small town on the edge of a huge Finnish forest. He was a very good hunter. People in the area knew him for being able to find and kill even the most elusive animals. Matti grew up hearing stories about Ajatar, the bad spirit of the forest. But like many young men, he thought these stories were just old wives' tales meant to scare kids. Matti went hunting one fall day when the leaves were going golden, and the air was getting cool. The prized white elk was said to walk freely in the middle of the forest, so he planned to go deeper into the forest than ever before. People older than him in town told him not to, but Matti was sure of his skills and knew a lot about the bush.

He went deeper into the woods and slowly stopped hearing the birds and small animals that he was used to hearing. From thin to thick, the trees in the forest got larger and more twisted. Shadows moved around the edges of his field of vision, and there was an odd quiet in the woods. He didn't stop because he was sure the white elk was close. As the day went on, Matti began to feel nervous. He couldn't get rid of the weird feeling in the forest. Someone looked at him, he thought. He was getting further into the bush with each step, but he didn't know what was there. It was hard for him to find his way because the trees looked like they were changing and moving.

Matti suddenly felt cold. The air smelled bad, as if something was going bad or someone was sick. In the old stories, it was said that Ajatar's breath could make people sick. This made him feel scared for the first time. He suddenly realized that he had gone into Ajatar's land by accident. As night fell, strange sounds could be heard in the forest. Matti heard sounds like snakes moving and saw flashes of movement in the dark. His mind was full of pictures of Ajatar, the woman who looked like a snake and had hair like writhing snakes. Trying to calm down, he told himself that it was all in his head, but he knew deep down that it wasn't true.

Matti could feel his strength being taken away all night. He got a fever, and his whole body hurt. He remembered the stories about how Ajatar could make people sick with just a look. Was the devil in the forest after him? He tried very hard to stay awake because he was scared of what would happen if he fell asleep in this scary forest. When dawn came, Matti was in a small area. He had never seen a circle with such an old, broken tree in the middle of it before. The branches were bent like snakes, and the wood looked like it was full of life from another world. She was sure that this was Ajatar's tree, the source of her power in the jungle.

Matti decided to try to get away one last time, getting stronger as he did so. He thought of a charm that his grandmother had taught him. It was a prayer for the forest guards to keep evil spirits away. He begged for help while his lips were shaking. He thought, for some reason, that the open door was letting a warm breeze in. The heavy mood eased, and Matti could feel some of his strength coming back. When he looked up, he saw a group of birds falling from the sky. Their songs broke the strange silence of Ajatar's forest.

The birds flew around Matti, making a shield to protect him. They led him through the tree-lined paths in the forest and away from the clearing. I saw Matti go after them. He felt hopeful for the first time since he got lost. It was interesting to see how the forest changed as Matti moved through it... The scary, dark trees gave way to woods that looked more like home. The air got better, and he could hear the sound of the trees again. Matti finally came out from behind the trees after what seemed like hours. He was on the edge of his town.

The people were thrilled when Matti came back. After three days, he hadn't been seen, and many people thought Ajatar had taken him over for good. Matti told his story, talking about his run-in with Ajatar's power and how he almost got away. Matti never went deep into the forest by himself again after that. He became an elder in the village and used his knowledge to warn young hunters about the scary things that lived deep in the woods. In the village, the story of Matti's meeting with Ajatar was passed down from generation to generation around the fire.

The town continued to be careful with the forest, only taking what they needed and always leaving gifts at the edge of the forest. For as long as they were polite, they thought Ajatar would stay in her lands and keep the village safe from her bad influence. After many years, when Matti was very old, he would sometimes stand at the edge of the forest and look into it. He would never forget meeting Ajatar, the evil ghost of the woods. The old stories were more than just stories to him. They were lessons and warnings that came from the close link between the Finns and the wild, mysterious forests that were all around them.

Matti's story became an important part of local legend. It showed clearly how powerful and dangerous Ajatar was. People were reminded of how thin the line is between the real world and the world of spirits and how important it is to respect nature's old forces. The story of Ajatar, a dark but important part of Finnish folklore, lived on through this story.

Some researchers think that Ajatar is like characters from other Nordic and Baltic myths. For instance, she is a lot like the Scandinavian Huldra, which is a dangerous but attractive wild spirit. Ajatar, on the other hand, was created by Finns because she was linked to disease and looked like a snake. In Finnish culture, Ajatar stands for the wild and dangerous parts of nature. In the past, Finns put much value on the nearby woods. Woods were dangerous because of wild animals, rough terrain, and the chance of getting lost. But they were also a good place to get food, fuel, and building materials.

The Ajatar character took on these fears, giving them a real shape that people could name and try to avoid in some ways. In Finnish society, believing in Ajatar and other ghosts like her was useful. Stories about Ajatar would teach people, especially kids, how dangerous it is to go too far into the forest by yourself. They told people to be careful when going into the woods and respect nature.

Along with the spread of Christianity in Finland, people began to think different things. More and more, it became clear that Ajatar and other forest spirits were devils or people who worked for the devil. But people in the countryside were scared of Ajatar for hundreds of years, and people in some small places that were far away still believed in her well into the 20th century.

HIISI: TRICKSTER SPIRIT IN THE FOREST

B Before Christianity came to Finland, there were trickster spirits in the country's woods. They were called Hiisi. Not just a few trees, these were holy places where the line between the real world and the world of ghosts became less thick. One of these Hiisi was deep in a forest, a long way from the next town. This spirit was different from the others nearby. A small clearing was surrounded by old trees with twisted roots and branches that reached out in all directions. In the middle was a big rock. Its surface was smooth because wind and rain had worn it down over the years. There was something powerful about this air that made the hairs on the back of your neck stand up.

A young, mighty god named Tapio lived in the deep forest. Tapio had always had a special bond with the woods, as his name comes from the god of the forest. He had gone with the village leaders to the sacred grove since he was a child and watched with wide eyes as they left gifts of food, drink, and hand-made items at the base of the big rock. As Hiisi got bigger, Tapio learned how to do things right when he went into his area. Always leave a gift when the hunting was good, and never, ever make fun of the holy grove. That's what he learned from growing up in the forest.

At this point, Tapio was a skilled lone hunter, but he still felt drawn to the holy grove, even when he wasn't there. He felt at ease and relaxed among the old trees. It was like Hiisi's spirit was happy to see him. He didn't know that his link to this place would be put to the test in ways he never thought possible. The villagers always had the holy grove in their lives, no matter the seasons or the years. It was a mysterious, powerful, and wise place from long ago that reminded people of how deeply they were connected to the land they lived on. But change was on the way, brought by winds from far away. It would make them question everything they thought they knew about Hiisi and the holy places their ancestors had visited.

Tapio met a strange old man one day while he was hunting deep in the forest. The stranger appeared out of nowhere, and his eyes were filled with a knowledge that seemed to come from another world. He told Tapio that times were changing and that it was important to remember the old ways, even though new ideas were coming into being. Tapio thought about what the old man had said for a long time after they had met.

He kept thinking that this meeting was different from the others and might have been Hiisi's way of telling him something. People in town didn't believe him when he told them about the meeting because they were scared. As more people in the town became Christians, their views on the sacred grove changed in a big way. People began to fear and avoid what used to be a place of prayer. People began to talk about scary ghosts living in the grove and waiting to grab visitors who weren't paying attention.

Fewer and fewer gifts were left at the big rock, and people who still followed the old ways did so in secret. The roads to the grove, which used to be well-kept, got overgrown. It looked like nature was trying to hide the holy spot from people. Tapio felt sad when he saw these changes. He had a different feeling in the trees around him. It looked like Hiisi's spirit was running away into the wild, away from scared and doubtful people. Strange things began to happen in the village.

Unexpectedly, crops failed, animals got sick, and hunters came back empty-handed from places that had always been rich. Many people thought that these bad things happened because Hiisi was angry and punished them for giving up their old ways. Others saw it as proof that the preachers were right when they said that the forest spirits were evil.

The village became even more divided. People who still believed in the old ways said they should go back to the holy grove and make peace with Hiisi. The new believers said they should destroy the wood to get rid of the evil they thought lived there. Tapio was getting more and more uneasy because he was in the middle of this fight. Deep down, he knew that the truth about Hiisi was more complicated than anyone thought. His mind kept going back to the old man's words, which told him to find the truth for himself. Tensions in the village were about to break, so Tapio made a choice. He was going to go deep into the bush, to the centre of Hiisi's territory, and find out what the old spirit really was. He had no idea that this quest would lead to big changes in his town as well as his own life.

As more and more strange things happened in the village, people became more afraid and suspicious. Animals got sick, crops died in the fields, and hunters came back from the forest without any goods. Many people thought that these bad things were happening because Hiisi was punishing them for giving up the old ways. Some people saw it as proof that the forest spirits were evil, just like the preachers had said they would be.

Tapio chose to do something because he was worried about the fighting in his community and the pain of his people. He was going to go deep into the bush to meet Hiisi and find out what really happened. Even though both Christians and people who still believed in the old ways told him not to go on his quest, Tapio got ready for it.

Tapio went to see the town blacksmith before leaving. In Finnish tradition, iron was thought to protect against ghosts and other supernatural beings. The blacksmith made Tapio a unique knife and blessed it with old magic and protection. In Finnish mythology, a bit of rowan wood, some salt, and a small pouch of graveyard dirt are all things that are thought to keep evil away. Tapio also got these things.

Tapio went deeper into the bush and saw that the paths he knew had changed. The trees looked taller, and their arms looked like they were reaching out to grab something. Sounds from the woods were strange. He wasn't able to place any of the sounds of the wind talking or the rustling in the low plants. The young hunter had a lot happen to him on his trip. He met a group of bad forest ghosts known as maahiset. They tried to confuse him with false tracks and illusions. Tapio tricked them by giving them a small gift and treating them with respect because he knew how things were done in the past.

Then, he came to a fast-moving river that looked like it would be impossible to cross. When Apio thought of old stories, he asked Vetehinen, the water spirit, for help. Then, out of nowhere, a log appeared in the water and calmed it down. More into Hiisi's area, Tapio ran into the worst trouble he had yet. Ajattara, which are evil spirits, tried to confuse and scare him when he found himself in a dark, foggy place. In Finnish folklore, these spirits are often thought of as evil women who tried to lead Tapio to his death. But Tapio wasn't fooled—he had an iron knife and was set on winning.

Hiisi was more than a place or a single thing, Tapio learned. There were many natural and magical forces in the idea, which made it hard to understand.

He realized that Hiisi's change in the eyes of the people in his village had less to do with Hiisi itself and more to do with how people saw and feared her. After what seemed like days of travel, Tapio finally got to the centre of Hiisi's country. Here, the forest opened up into a large clearing that looked a lot like the sacred grove close to his town. With their branches tangled high up, old trees made a natural church. A big, worn-out stone altar in the middle looked a lot like the rock in the village's grove.

As Tapio walked up to the altar, he could feel the weight of all the people who had come before him, looking for the truth and balance with nature. He knew that what happened next would affect not only his life but also the lives of everyone in his town. In the middle of Hiisi's domain, Tapio stood in front of an old temple. The air around him started to shimmer. Every tree and blade of grass in the forest seemed to come to life with an energy from another world. Someone showed up in front of him out of the blue. There was nothing scary or nice about it. It looked like the forest itself.

It wasn't in any way good or bad; it was just a natural force that didn't care what people think is right or wrong. It looked like an old man sometimes, with a beard of grass and eyes that were the size of swimming pools. At other times, it looked like a huge elk with horns that reached the sky. At other times, it looked like a mist that was moving around and didn't have a clear shape. Hiisi and Tapio talked to each other not with words but with a number of visions and feelings. Tapio knew the history of how his people had treated the forest: how they used to respect and honour it, how they kept the balance, and how that balance had been thrown off.

His town was having bad luck because people had given up on the old ways of living in peace with nature, not because they were being punished. People had forgotten how to work the land the old way, not because Hiisi was crazy. That's why the crops failed. Because the forest was out of whack, the animals got sick. He learned that Hiisi and the idea it stood for kept nature in order and kept old knowledge safe. The old ways could be very helpful when everyone agreed with them. But when people try to control or ignore nature, it can be seen as a scary force.

Tapio was shown by the spirit that Hiisi's change from a liked idea to a feared being showed how people were changing how they related to nature. They changed how they thought about Hiisi as they stopped seeing themselves as part of nature and started seeing themselves as separate from it. Tapio learned from Hiisi how important it is always to have a mix of new and old things. It showed him that instead of completely rejecting new ideas, he should combine them with what his ancestors knew. Hiisi wasn't against growth, but they did not like how it often made people lose touch with nature.

Tapio was back to being alone in front of the altar after the images ended. He wasn't the same person who came into the grove, however. With this new knowledge, he could better understand Hiisi and how important it was to keep the world in order. With Tapio's help, the town began to change over time. They left gifts in the holy woods again, not because they were scared, but because they cared about the environment. They learned to value both their new Christian beliefs and the natural world. It was a win-win situation for everyone.

People started to feel better when they connected with nature and learned old things. This made the town's bad luck go away. It was good for crops again, animals got better, and hunters did well in the wild. People looked for Tapio because they thought he was smart and knew a lot about how the real world and the Hiisi world fit together. It was something he taught others his whole life, and he made sure others learned from what he had taught them.

Hiisi's story changed once more. No longer was it about a scary or good god. It was about an important part of nature and how important it is to live in harmony with it. The story of Tapio and his quest became part of the past of the village. It made them think of how strong their old ideas were and how smart the trees were.

MIELIKKI AND HER NINE SONS

People know about the Finnish legendary character Mielikki. She rules over the woods and the hunt. Tapio, the forest god, married her. Finnic stories often talk about Mielikki as a being who heals and watches over animals. But "Mielikki and Her Nine Sons" isn't really about the goddess Mielikki. Instead, it's a version of a common type of folktale called "The Three Golden Children" (ATU 707). People who speak Finno-Ugric languages in Russia and Finland have stories like this.

When this story is told in Finnish, it usually starts with three sisters talking about how smart they are. The younger sister makes an amazing claim: she says she will have nine children over the course of three pregnancies, and each one will be unique. This talk is heard by a king, who then chooses to marry the youngest sister. The queen gets pregnant soon after they get married. But the king's absence during the births sets off a chain of bad things that happen.

When this story is told in Finnish, it goes in a different direction than what you might expect from a Mielikki story. The story is not about a hunt but about the birth of the unusual children and the betrayal that followed. A mystery midwife shows up when the queen gives birth. According to some stories, this midwife is actually Syöjätär, a bad person from Finnish folklore. Syöjätär, or sometimes the queen's jealous older sisters, takes the babies and turns them into animals.

Three times, this change takes place, representing the three pregnancies the queen had promised. It is said that each time, the queen gave birth to animals instead of the golden children who were promised. When the king finds out that his wife gave birth to animals instead of the magical children he had promised, he gets very angry. Most versions of the story say that he throws her out to sea in a barrel to punish the queen.

The queen does, however, save her smallest child from the last pregnancy. They are all thrown into the water together in the barrel. They wash up on an island after a dangerous trip. The child who was saved grows very quickly on this island. When he's old enough, he asks his mom to use her milk to make nine cakes. These cakes are very important for his plan to save his brothers.

The framework of this story is different from what you might expect from a story about a forest goddess, even though it is called Mielikki. There are themes of betrayal, survival, and the victory of the truth that runs through many folktales around the world. Mielikki's story and that of her nine sons take a strange turn when we follow the queen and her youngest child on their trip. They are thrown out to sea in a barrel and somehow make it to a mystery island where they land. They decide to live on this island, which is also where the young prince grows very quickly and becomes strong and smart.

As the prince grows up, he will ask his mom to make nine special cakes with her milk. There are a lot of these cakes out there. The prince has to save his brothers. After making the cakes, the young prince leaves on his trip. He sees a bird on the path. He is nice and lets the bird live so it won't get hurt. It feels good for the bird to help the prince. The bird wants the prince to be nice. The bird flies the prince across the ocean to a different place. That place will hold something very interesting for him.

In this new land, the prince finds his seven brothers. They don't look like people, however. They are stuck as birds because of a strange curse that changed them. Many folktales have this change as a main theme. It generally means losing your humanity or finishing a sentence. With the special cakes his mother made and the knowledge of what happened to his brothers, the prince starts to break the curse. Details about how he does this aren't given in the sources we have access to, but the cakes likely play a big part in the brothers turning back into humans.

A new order is set up when the curse is broken, and the brothers turn back into humans. As the Finnish forest goddess Mielikki, her presence can be felt in the background, even though the story doesn't say that she has a direct role in this part of it. Now that the brothers are back together, they need to deal with what happened and figure out where they belong in the world. They probably learned important lessons about the value of family, the effects of anger and betrayal, and the strength of sticking with something even when it gets hard.

In many variations of the same story, the queen's innocence is proven, and she is reunited with her husband, the king. Most stories have bad people who split up the kids and changed them to get in trouble. But the specifics depend on the tale. Things should get better in the forest realm by the end of the story. It taught us to be kind to nature, spend time with family, and think about how our actions affect other people. This story is an interesting piece of Finnish storytelling. It's about family, change, and forgiveness, among other things. It has parts that are like many European fairy tales and parts that are only found in Finnish myths and stories.

ILMARINEN

Ilmarinen is one of the most famous figures in Finnish mythology. He is said to have been very skilled and had divine power. Ilmarinen is regarded as both a god of creation and a god of the weather. He is known as the "eternal smith." His history goes back to old Finnish folklore, where he is seen as one of Kaleva's sons and the mythical ancestor of the Finnish people. It is said that Ilmarinen was born in the middle of the night to a mother called Iro-neito, but no one knows for sure. Because he comes from a holy family, he has amazing powers and is very important in Finnish myths.

As a god of artistry, Ilmarinen has the best skills in the world. People know him for being able to make almost anything, from everyday tools to magical items. He knew a lot about the elements, as shown by his most famous piece, The Dome of the Sky. The story goes that Ilmarinen made the heavens, which are the skies above the world. Ilmarinen is known for more than just making things. He is also linked to nature events. People think he came up with the idea for the auroras, which are the dancing lights that light up the northern sky. The bright colours of dawn and dusk are also his work. He used his artistic skills to paint the sky.

He is even more important to Finnish society because he is in the Kalevala, which is Finland's national epic. Elias Lönnrot put together this collection of myths and folktales. It includes Ilmarinen's stories and shows how important he is to Finnish society. The story of Ilmarinen making the Sampo is one of the most well-known in Finnish folklore. That's how good he was at making things and how he changed things for his people. Many people wanted it because they knew it would make them rich for life. At the start of the story, Väinämöinen, the wise old man, is in danger. Louhi, the smart and strong witch who ruled Pohjola in the North, had him in her grip. Louhi saw a chance to get something useful.

He told Louhi a big promise because he was so eager to be free. He told her that Ilmarinen, the best blacksmith in the land, would make her the Sampo. This is the Sampo, a magical item that holds a lot of power and wonder. Louhi was interested in having such a magical thing, so he agreed to let Väinämöinen go as long as this condition was met. Soon after he got back, Väinämöinen gave Ilmarinen the job. Ilmarinen was hesitant at first because he knew it would be hard to make such a powerful device. Ilmarinen finally agreed to go to Pohjola because he knew how important the job was and that it was his role to help Väinämöinen.

Ilmarinen had a hard time on his way to the northern realm. Pohjola was known for having a harsh temperature and strange, often dangerous, people living there. Ilmarinen was holy and driven, so he was able to get through these issues. When Ilmarinen got to Pohjola, he was given the tough job of making the Sampo. People said that the Sampo was a magical mill that could make enough flour, salt, and money to last forever. Ilmarinen would have to really work hard and think outside the box to make it.

Then Ilmarinen got to work setting up his forge and gathering the things he would need. There were many steps to making the Sampo. Every day and night, Ilmarinen worked hard to make things. He used his unmatched crafting skills and strong magic. The magic thing moved around in his forge, making the air around it shake with power. He had to show how good he was when he built the Sampo. He had to deal with a lot of setbacks and issues that needed him to think outside the box and stay determined. The Sampo was magical, so that normal forging methods wouldn't work on it. Ilmarinen had to learn a lot about both magic and forging.

Ilmarinen gave the Sampo amazing abilities as he worked on it. People said that one side of the Sampo could grind grain, another could grind salt, and a third could make gold. The Sampo was very valuable and sought after because it could be used both in real life and to make magic money. Before he was done, Ilmarinen seemed to have worked on the Sampo for a very long time. It was clear from what Ilmarinen made how skilled he was and how strong Finnish folklore is. It had beautiful, intricate patterns on its surface, and magical energy pulsed through it.

When the Sampo was finished, Ilmarinen gave it to Louhi. The witch was thrilled when she saw the magical mill and knew right away that it could make her land very wealthy. She agreed to take the Sampo, keeping the deal she made with Väinämöinen. However, Sampo's story doesn't end when it is made and given to the person. When the thing was used to cause trouble and have fun in later stories, it became an important part of Finnish lore. It was wanted by many because they knew it would make them rich for life.

This made tasks and fights all about getting it. When Ilmarinen made the Sampo, it became official that he was the best blacksmith in Finnish lore. It not only showed how smart he was with technology but also how truly amazing the things he could make were. He became even more powerful among the Finnish gods and heroes because of this. The story of how the Sampo came to be also shows how complicated the relationships and deals that run through many Finnish myths. It shows how the actions of one hero (Väinämöinen) can cause things to happen that need the skills and help of another (Ilmarinen), creating a complex web of myths and legends that are all linked.

Ilmarinen experiences both happiness and sadness when she finds love. Through his trip, we can see that the Smith god has both divine and human emotions. His thoughts turned to love after making the Sampo, and he set his sights on Louhi's daughter, the Maiden of Pohjola. It wasn't easy to court the

Maiden of Pohjola. Louhi, being the sneaky witch she is, gave Ilmarinen a list of jobs that seemed impossible to do to show how good a suitor he was. These tests were meant to see how strong and skilled Ilmarinen was, as well as how determined and smart he was.

Ilmarinen had to plough a field full of vipers for the first job. The divine smith didn't give up. He used his godly strength to make a plough out of gold and silver. After that, he was told to catch the underworld's big bear and Tuoni, the god of death,'s dog. But Ilmarinen's imagination won out this time. He was brave and good at being a blacksmith, which let him do these things. Louhi told Ilmarinen to catch the big fish that lived in the river Tuonela, which is also known as the "land of the dead."

This job turned out to be the hardest, but Ilmarinen was determined and had skills that no one else had. He succeeded where others would have failed. Ilmarinen was able to marry the Maiden of Pohjola after he did these impossible things. In the epic poem The Kalevala, their wedding is described as a big party with eating and drinking that went on for days. Ilmarinen seemed to be completely happy, and his search for love was over.

His happiness in marriage did not last long, however. In a cruel turn of events that shows how legendary stories are often true, Ilmarinen's wife died too soon. Ilmarinen was so sad about his loss that it drove him to try something quite amazing: making a new bride out of gold and silver. Ilmarinen worked hard to make a beautiful wife with his special skills. He helped her get in shape for a long time. When he was done, the golden girl looked very pretty and sparkled. He quickly found out that even though it looked nice, it wasn't a real friend because it didn't have love or life.

The golden wife didn't make him feel loved or cared for because she was cold to the touch. It is a moving story about Ilmarinen's golden wife that shows that even God's power can't change what's going on in the heart. It shows that metal can't make true love and friendship, no matter how good the person who made it is. He did brave things to finish impossible tasks and sad things to look for his lost love. His search for love shows how complicated he is. He's a holy being who can do great things, but he's still a person.

Hey. In Finnish folklore, Ilmarinen is both good and bad, which makes her interesting and easy to relate to—stories from all over the world about love, loss, and friendship. Ilmarinen was a different person before he fell in love. In many other stories, he remained very important because he was one of the most important people in Finnish folklore. One of

Ilmarinen's most important later experiences was his part in the raid to get back the Sampo.

Even though Ilmarinen made this magical item, he worked with Väinämöinen, Lemminkäinen, Louhi and the people of Pohjola to get it back. During this quest, there was a huge fight at sea, and the Sampo was lost. It was said that the pieces that it broke into would still bring wealth to the places where they washed up. He was so good at what he did that it was better than anything else made on Earth. People thought he made things in heaven, which made him look like a god who made everything.

He is said to have made the Dome of the Sky, which was a huge job that proved he was in charge of everything. Some people also said that he made the moon and stars and put them in the sky to light up the night. Ilmarinen was more than just a great blacksmith, as shown by the things that came back from space. The world changed because of him. His importance in Finnish mythology is shown by the fact that he can make things from both land and heaven.

Ilmarinen often worked with other heroes from Finnish mythology during his many journeys. His work with Väinämöinen and Lemminkäinen on different tasks shows how linked Finnish stories are. Because Ilmarinen was so good at crafting, he was often able to combine his skills with those of his fellow heroes, which helped them solve problems that seemed hard to solve.

Ilmarinen's later adventures show that he is still a complicated person. He is a powerful god who can change the universe, but he also gets involved in very human fights and quests. The fact that he is still important in Finnish mythology shows how appealing his character is and how rich Finnish folklore is as a storytelling tradition.

JOUKAHAINEN: REVIVAL OF VÄINÄMÖINEN

In Finnish mythology, Joukahainen is a central person. The national epic poem, the Kalevala, makes him the most famous character. This figure, who is young and cocky, represents both the spirit of cockiness in youth and the bad things that happen when you question what everyone else thinks. Joukahainen's story comes from Karelia's rich oral traditions. It has been told from generation to generation until it was included in the works of Elias Lönnrot in the 19th century.

Finnish folklore uses Joukahainen to show the image of the cocky young person and to warn others about the risks of being too sure of themselves and not respecting their elders. The story of his meetings with the wise shaman Väinämöinen is one of the most dramatic and important in Finnish mythology.

Joukahainen is a complicated figure in the Kalevala. He is shown to be both a victim of his pride and the cause of important events. He did something that changed not only his own life but also the lives of other important people in the story, like his sister Aino and the main character Väinämöinen.

Early in Kalevala, Joukahainen invites Väinämöinen to a contest to see how much they know and how well they can sing magic. This is the most popular story about Joukahainen. This challenge is the most important part of Joukahainen's part in the story, and it sets the stage for what happens next.

The competition between Joukahainen and Väinämöinen is a test of their skill and intelligence. Joukahainen is sure of his skills and brags about how much he knows about how the world was made and natural events. But Väinämöinen's magic music and wise words are much better. Väinämöinen's songs start to directly affect Joukahainen, making him sink into a swamp as the contest goes on.

When Joukahainen realizes he has lost, he begs for forgiveness. In order to get away, he offers Väinämöinen many valuable things, but the old wise man turns them all down. Joukahainen is desperate, so he offers Väinämöinen the hand of his sister Aino in marriage. The old man accepts, and Joukahainen is freed from the pond.

The promise that Aino made to Väinämöinen turns out to be very bad. When Aino finds out about her brother's promise, she is upset about the idea of marrying the old Väinämöinen. She decides to drown herself instead of marrying this man she doesn't want to, which adds to the sadness of Joukahainen's hasty actions.

Soon after, Joukahainen tries to get back at Väinämöinen because he feels bad about losing and angry about losing his sister. He sneaks up on the old man with a crossbow. However, his plan fails, solidifying his place as Väinämöinen's enemy in the epic.

Scholars and folklorists have come up with many different ways to understand Joukahainen's character because she is full of symbols. He's not just one character in a story; he's a symbol of bigger problems and themes in Finnish society and people in general.

The competition between Joukahainen and Väinämöinen can be seen as a symbol of the clash between old-fashioned knowledge and new ideas from young people. "Väinämöinen" means old, tried-and-true knowledge, and "Joukahainen" means new, fresh ideas that haven't been tried yet. This fight shows how generations always have a hard time finding the best way to keep rituals alive while also being open to new things.

The way the story is told in the Kalevala makes Joukahainen different from Väinämöinen. He is very different from Väinämöinen, who is older, more patient, and much smarter. He is impatient, young, and doesn't know much. This difference makes Väinämöinen the story's main character and shows how great he is. Joukahainen is best known for his part in the Kalevala. However, his character has deeper roots in Finnish culture and shows up in different ways in different places and traditions.

Some area folktales have different versions of Joukahainen's character, which has different traits or roles. In some stories, he is shown in a more sympathetic light as a young shaman with great skills who only messed up by facing someone much stronger than him. Before the Kalevala was written down, stories about Joukahainen were told orally from one family to the next. The different cultural backgrounds of Finland and Karelia can be seen in these local tales about the singing contest and what happened after it.

Joukahainen is also in other types of Finnish folk poems besides the Kalevala. In some poems, he is a more important character, going on more travels and meeting more mythical creatures. These poems help us understand Joukahainen's role in Finnish mythology in a bigger picture.

Joukahainen's personality is a lot like that of other characters in Nordic and European folklore. He stands for young people going too far, like Icarus in Greek mythology. His feud with Väinämöinen is like battles between younger and older gods in different pantheons. This is a common theme in Indo-European mythology.

People in Finland still talk about and think about Joukahainen's story, but they do so in new ways and with new meanings. This person has shaped a lot of writing, art, and music. Finnish painters and sculptors have shown the singing fight, and modern writers have written about it from Joukahainen's point of view. In present-day Finland, Joukahainen's story is often used to show how dangerous pride can be and how important it is to value experience. It helps me remember how important it is always to learn and be humble.

He has been involved in a lot of different pop culture, from comic books to rock operas. Many of the time, these versions change his personality to make him more likeable to modern viewers.

TALE OF KULLERVO

T he story of Kullervo starts with a nasty fight between two brothers, Untamo and Kalervo. This struggle sets off the terrible things that happen next. Untamo attacks Kalervo's group and kills almost everyone because he is angry and jealous. But Kalervo's pregnant wife lives through the massacre. The wife of Kalervo has twins while they are being held captive. Their names are Kullervo and Wanona. Kullervo has been different from a very young age. He is incredibly strong and has a fierce spirit that can't be broken. Even though these traits are amazing, they often cause trouble and damage for those around him.

Untamo tries to kill Kullervo more than once because he is afraid the child will get back at him. He tries to kill the boy by drowning, setting him on fire, and hanging him, but Kullervo always makes it through, thanks to some magic that protects him. This string of failed murder efforts makes Kullervo even more angry and makes him want to get revenge. As Kullervo gets older, Untamo decides to keep him as a slave rather than try to kill him again and fail. Kullervo is put to work on different jobs, but the boy's extreme strength and lack of care always end badly. When Kullervo is given a job, he destroys boats, trees, and walls.

Untamo finally sells Kullervo as a slave because he is tired of Kullervo's destructive behaviour. Ilmarinen, a skilled blacksmith from Finnish legend, buys Kullervo. Kullervo's life doesn't get better in Ilmarinen's home. He doesn't get along with others and has trouble getting things done without making a mess. When Ilmarinen's wife bakes a stone into Kullervo's bread because she doesn't like how he's acting, things start to change. The knife that Kullervo has from his father is the only thing that reminds him of his family. When he bites into the bread, it breaks on the secret stone. This event wakes up Kullervo's dormant magical skills and makes him want to get even.

Kullervo calls wild animals with his new magical skills because he is furious about losing the only family treasure and being treated badly all the time. These animals are sent to kill Ilmarinen's wife by attacking her. He leaves the smith's house after that. Kullervo had a hard childhood and didn't fit in with other kids. This part of the story shows how he first got his magical skills. This makes him want to get even, which leads to the terrible events that follow. Kullervo leaves Ilmarinen's house and goes to find his family. He is shocked and glad to hear that his parents and siblings are still alive. The people were able to hide near the border of Lapland after Untamo took them out.

Kullervo is happy for a short time, however. Along the way home, he meets a young woman in the forest. Kullervo seduces her without knowing who she is. Sadly, they find out later that they are brother and sister. His sister drowns herself in a river because she is too sad and ashamed to live another day. When Kullervo finds out this terrible truth, he loses it. He wants to get even with Untamo, the man who killed his family and made him work as a slave for years.

Kullervo's parents and other family members try to stop him from going down this path of revenge by telling him it won't work and bad things could happen. But Kullervo doesn't listen because he is angry and has magical powers. Kullervo sets out on his plan to get even. He calls on mysterious forces to call in wild animals and natural disasters. Kullervo attacks Untamo's tribe with this scary army under his direction. He doesn't care about anyone else and kills Untamo and destroys everything in his way.

When Kullervo gets paid back, he goes home and finds that his house is empty and deserted. He has lost everything—his family, his sister, and now his home. This makes him feel helpless. He kills himself because he can't handle the bad things that have happened to him and the things he has done. He goes into the forest to the exact spot where he wooed his sister without meaning to. He picks death over a life full of pain and guilt and falls on his sword.

At the end of his story, Väinämöinen, the wise old man, warned Kullervo. People should not be mean to their children, and it is very important to care for and teach them with kindness and care. Because of Kullervo, Finnish writing and stories have changed a great deal. People have always had ideas about fate, getting even, and what happens after you do something. Different writers, including famous ones like J.R.R. Tolkien, have written different versions of the story. Kullervo's story is a strong warning about how painful it can be to get even and how important family and identity are. It's still a big part of Finnish society, and it helps us understand how people are and how morals can be tricky.

THE SWAN OF TUONELA

Finns believe that Tuonela is the place where the dead live. The dead live there in the dark. This scary, dark place is cut off from the living world by a deep, black river. Tuonela is ruled by the goddess Tuonetar and her husband, the god of death, Tuoni. The scenery in Tuonela is dark and scary. Here, the sun and moon never shine, so the land is always dark. The black river runs through the middle of Tuonela. Its water is fast and dangerous. The legendary Swan of Tuonela lives in this river. It is a beautiful bird that glides quietly through the dark water.

Folklore in Finland says that after they die, the dead go to Tuonela. They have to cross the dangerous river, and Tuoni's daughter often steers a boat that helps them. Once the dead arrive in Tuonela, they walk around as shadowy ghosts. Their fate is the same no matter what they do in life. A lot of Finnish myths and legends are about Tuonela. In the epic poem Kalevala, for example, heroes sometimes go into this forbidden land.

Lemminkäinen is a well-known hero in Finnish myth. He is known for being brave and careless. In a dramatic quest that ends with his death and revival, his story is linked to the world of Tuonela. At the beginning of the story, Lemminkäinen wants to marry one of Louhi's daughters. Louhi is the powerful mistress of the northland Pohjola. For Lemminkäinen, Louhi gives him three impossible jobs. The last and most dangerous one is to catch or kill the Swan of Tuonela.

Even though this is a dangerous job, Lemminkäinen still sets out for Tuonela. His trip takes him through dangerous places and gives him much trouble along the way. As he gets closer to the edge of the ground, it gets colder and darker. When Lemminkäinen gets to the black river, he meets Tuoni's blind son, who is watching over the entrance to Tuonela. He tries to cross the river and get close to the Swan even though everyone tells him not to.

Lemminkäinen wades through the dark water and sees the pretty Swan fly off into the mist. Sadly, bad things happen before he can get to the bird. When the blind son of Tuoni hears that Lemminkäinen is nearby, he throws a poisoned spear at him. When the spear hits its mark, Lemminkäinen dies and falls to the ground. The flow of the water takes his broken and torn body away. It goes down into the water and rests on the rocks below. Lemminkainen's quest didn't work out, and he died.

His spirit is now stuck in the place he was trying to take over. Of course, this is not the end of the story. When Lemminkäinen's mother thinks that something bad has happened to her son, she starts a frantic search. As she goes around the world, she asks every living thing where her son is. The sun finally shows her that Lemminkäinen is dead in the Tuonela River. So that she can save her son, Lemminkäinen's mother goes to the smith god Ilmarinen and asks him to make a big rake with steel tines and a copper handle. Using this tool, she goes to Tuonela and starts the hard work of getting her son's body out of the river.

She carefully puts Lemminkäinen's body back together on the bank of the river, finding pieces of it as she goes. However, Lemminkäinen is still dead despite her best efforts and strong healing spells. Lemminkäinen's mother sends a bee to the halls of the great god Ukko to get a drop of honey that has the power to bring life. Putting this magical honey on Lemminkäinen's body brings him back to life, ending one of the most dramatic stories in Finnish lore.

The tale of Lemminkäinen and the Swan of Tuonela is a very important part of Finnish culture and folklore. A Finnish story shows how strong mother love can be, how dangerous pride can be, and how very little space there is between life and death. He will never be the same again, though, after his time in Tuonela. After coming back from the dead, he goes back to the real world. The Swan of Tuonela, on the other hand, sleeps through the night on the dark river.

It stands for what can't be touched and the line between life and death. This story has had a big impact on Finnish art and culture. "The Swan of Tuonela" from Jean Sibelius's Lemminkäinen Suite may have been inspired by this song the most. In this scary piece, Sibelius uses the sad sound of the English horn to represent the Swan's song, which makes me think of Tuonela's sad mood.

Important parts of Finnish shamanic customs are also shown in the story. The trip Lemminkäinen took to Tuonela could be seen as a shamanic quest, and his resurrection could be seen as a shamanic way of getting his soul back. The Swan of Tuonela stands for the wall between the worlds of the living and the dead in Finnish folklore. The fact that it is in the dark river is a reminder of the secrets that only gods can understand. People are still interested in the story, and it has been used to spark new stories and art. For that reason, it is still an important part of Finnish culture history. It shows how Finnish mythology is used in everyday life.

SYÖJÄTÄR: SCARRY FINNISH MONSTER

In Finnish mythology, the Syöjätär is a scary monster that is also called the "Eateress." She is an ogress, which means she is linked to bad things, sickness, and dangerous pets. In many Finnish folk tales, Syöjätär is an important character. She acts like a mean mom or a bad guy, and the heroes have to beat her a lot of the time. Some people say that Syöjätär is a scary, ugly woman who can do magic. She can change into different animals and make them scary. She is sometimes shown as the mother and leader of snakes in stories. Her name, which means "she who eats," gives you an idea of how dangerous and hungry she is. The history of Syöjätär can be found in old Finnish "Magic Songs," which were collections of spells and incantations made by researchers in the 1800s. In these songs, the birth of Syöjätär is linked to a strange and magical event.

At the start of the story, Pohja (the North)'s wife, Louhiatar, gets pregnant in a strange way. A strong gust of wind knocks Louhiatar out one day while she is sleeping with her back to the wind. This magical conception makes the pregnancy hard and lasts a long time. It's been more than nine months, and now Louhiatar needs a place to give birth. It's hard for her to find a good spot until Ukko, the god of thunder, talks to her from above. They go to a shed with three corners in the dark land of Pohjola. The shed is in a swamp and faces the sea.

Louhiatar lives here with her nine boys and one daughter in a strange place. God and John the Baptist both tell her no when she tries to get them baptized. Louhiatar doesn't give up. She baptizes the kids herself and gives them names that mean different illnesses and bad luck. She doesn't name one of her boys because he was born without a mouth or eyes. These rivers are where Louhiatar sends this child. Many bad things are said to come from this unnamed son, such as sharp frosts, sorcerers, wizards, jealous people, and the animals called Syöjätärs.

This story tells how Syöjätär and her kind came to be. They were created when wind and a powerful northern being joined together. They were meant to bring bad luck and problems to the world of people. In Finnish folklore, Syöjätär is known for making many scary and unpleasant monsters. She is best known for making the snake, which is an important character in many Finnish stories. The stories say that Syöjätär made snakes out of her spit. She spat into the water one day as she walked along the shore. She spit on the ground, where the sun warmed it and the wind dried it. This is where the first snake came from.

According to Finnish culture, Syöjätär is also linked to making other animals that are seen as bad or dangerous. Some of these are dogs and lizards. She has a strong link to snakes because, in some stories, she is seen as the mother and leader of all snakes. Syöjätär is connected to more than just animals. It is also linked to the start and spread of many diseases. Many illnesses were thought to have magical causes in Finnish folk beliefs. Syöjätär was often blamed for this bad luck. So, in a spell against syphilis, the disease is called the "progeny of Syöjätär," which emphasizes her role as a disease-bringer.

The things that Syöjätär made show the fears and problems that ancient Finns had to deal with every day. Finns were really in danger from wild animals, dangerous plants, and strange illnesses because of the bad weather. People linked the dangers they saw around them to a single, evil being like Syöjätär so they could make sense of them and use magic and practices to stay safe.

In many Finnish folktales, the heroes have to beat or trick Syöjätär's creations as part of their journeys. In some stories, for example, the characters have to find ways to get rid of snakes or heal sicknesses that are linked to Syöjätär. Stories like these are often used to teach lessons about being brave and smart and how important it is to know things in order to get through life's problems.

The stories that Syöjätär made up remind us of how closely Finnish culture and nature are linked. They show how people had a complicated relationship with their surroundings. In Finland's woods and waters, beauty and danger often lived together.

CREATION OF THE WORLD

B efore the world as we know it, there was nothing there a long time ago. In this huge, dark area, there was only air and water. Ilmatar, the spirit of clean air, was the first to come down to this spot. People said she was the spirit of nature and the daughter of the sky. Ilmatar is called "Air Maiden" in Finnish. She got lonely in the sky, so she decided to go down to the clean water below. She went down to the ocean floor and stayed there for 700 years. She thought about how big the sea and the air were as she looked around at how empty it was.

While Ilmatar was on her float, the wind and water made her pregnant. She didn't give birth right away, however. She could have stayed on land, but she chose to stay on the water and drift for hundreds of years while carrying her child. Even though it was hard, she didn't give up because she knew something good was growing inside her. While Ilmatar sailed through the endless sea, the world had no shape. Mountain ranges, trees, and living things were not there, so it wasn't land. There were no stars in the sky, and neither the sun nor the moon shone on the gloom. Everything was ready to be born, just like the child inside Ilmatar.

Since Ilmatar was floating, the basic waters started to change because of her. The way she moved made the waves and currents in the water. In a world full of chaos, these small changes were the first signs of order. They were a taste of what was to come. On Ilmatar's journey through the primordial seas, there was more than just the journey itself. He was also changed on a psychic level. She was strong and patient for 700 years, which set the stage for the amazing things that happened next, which made the world and gave birth to the first man.

As Ilmatar kept floating on the water at the

beginning, a very interesting thing happened. An Ilmatar's knee could be seen above the water when a duck was looking for a place to nest. This looked like a good spot for the bird to land and build its nest. The duck made a new nest on Ilmatar's knee and put seven eggs there. Six of these eggs are made of gold, which means they are expensive and hard to find. The seventh egg is strong and will last a long time because it is made of iron. Ilmatar didn't move while the duck took care of its eggs because it didn't want to bother the duck or its nest.

For some reason, Ilmatar began to feel bad over time. It was so hot that she almost couldn't stand the eggs on her knee any longer. Ilmatar moved her leg quickly because the heat was too much for her. When she moved quickly, the eggs flew off her knee and fell into the deep water below. When the eggs hit the water as they fell, they broke. But something amazing happened instead of being destroyed. When eggshells were broken, they began to change. The bottoms of the shells turned into dirt, which was the first ground in the middle of the ocean that never ended. The sky's dome shape came from the tops of the shells rising.

Inside the eggs, too, things changed. The moon and stars were made from egg whites. At night, they were the first things that lit up the sky. Egg whites were used to make the sun, which warmed and lit up the new world. The cosmic egg gave birth to the world's parts in this way. They were amazed and happy to see this big change. She chose to swim through the water and use her body to make the new ground.

She swam in places with bays and currents. Where her foot touched the bottom, she made deep holes in the water. She built islands so she could keep her head above water. She changed the land around her as she moved. She shaped the shorelines with her hands, carved out the pathways with her fingers, and made pools for fish on the seafloor with her feet. Her view of the world became more clear and deep with each step she took.

It took a while for the Ilmatar to shape the earth's features as they made things carefully. Because of how she moved through the water, hills, rivers, lakes, and mountains were formed. The world was taking shape, changing from an empty place with no shape to a beautiful wide range of scenes. Ilmatar was pregnant with the first man's seed the whole time that the world was being made. The world she was building would soon be home to her child and everyone else who would live there after them.

After Ilmatar gave birth, her long pregnancy was finally over. The name of her beautiful child is Väinämöinen. Väinämöinen was a fully grown, wise old man when he came out, which is different from most kids. He was very smart and powerful from birth. This was the land that his mother, Ilmatar, made. Väinämöinen looked around and saw that the land was dead and empty, even though the sky and earth were there.

Väinämöinen got to work making this new world a living place. He went all over the land and used his magic and knowledge to make things grow and stay healthy. As he walked, plants began to grow there. He sang songs that were magical and made trees and flowers grow. Väinämöinen's work turned the empty land into a world full of life and wealth. There were new wildlife and plants on the land, as well as new fields and woods. He changed the world with strong chants and magic. These changes set up the way that life and the seasons work.

He healed people first and was very good at it. He was still making a big deal out of everything. He knew magic songs and helped shape the land, which made things better for people and showed them the way. Väinämöinen was the first person to ever be born on Earth in many Finnish stories. Väinämöinen made the world real, and now there will be many more myths and stories set there. These stories are what make up Finnish culture.

VÄINÄMÖINEN
IN POHJOLA

Our old and wise hero, Väinämöinen, set out to find a mate in the strange land of Pohjola. He tried to marry Aino before he went on his quest but failed. She sadly killed herself instead of getting married to the old man. Väinämöinen ran into trouble on his way to Pohjola. This surprised Väinämöinen because he was still mad about losing the first time. Väinämöinen fell into the water after being hit by an arrow from Joukahainen. He sank in the water for days until an eagle, grateful for past kindnesses, picked him up and brought him to the shore of Pohjola.

Väinämöinen met Louhi, the evil queen of the northern land, when he got to Pohjola. Her offer to help Väinämöinen get home was so sweet that she even said one of her girls would be his bride. Louhi was known for being sneaky. Her offer came with a catch, though: Väinämöinen had to make the Sampo, a very powerful magical item. He said that skilled blacksmith Ilmarinen would make the Sampo instead since he couldn't do it himself.

The Sampo wasn't like other things. To the person who owned it, it meant wealth and happiness because it could make salt, meal, and gold. Louhi asked for this strong thing in exchange for her daughter's hand in marriage. This set off a chain of events that would change the lives of both Kalevala and Pohjola. He went back to Kalevala to get help from Ilmarinen. The skilled blacksmith agreed to do the work because he was known for making one-of-a-kind items. The Ilmarinen went to Pohjola and asked him to help them make the Sampo. This magical piece of art moved Louhi, so she kept her promise and asked her daughter to marry him.

But the story took a turn that no one saw coming.

When Väinämöinen went back to Pohjola to claim his bride, Ilmarinen was also there to look for her. Ponokka's daughter got to pick between Ilmarinen and Väinämöinen, and she chose Ilmarinen. Louhi, who was always smart, gave Ilmarinen a long list of things that he had to do before he could marry her daughter. Some of these jobs were to plough a field full of vipers, catch the bear of Tuonela (the land of the dead), and catch a big pike from the river in the underworld. With the help of his future wife, Ilmarinen did these things well, which proved his worth and earned him the right to marry Louhi's daughter.

Pohjola became very wealthy when he built up and owned the Sampo. The magic mill always made money, which made the North's land strong and wealthy. After this turn of events, the people of Kalevala wanted to take the Sampo for themselves. This made Kalevala and Pohjola fight. People in the Kalevala have complicated relationships with the people who live in Pohjola. The story of the Sampo and the fight for the hand of Louhi's daughter shows this. In Finnish folklore, magical objects are very important. This shows that skill, both in making things and doing things that seem impossible, can decide your fate.

People in this story are jealous of the Sampo and want to steal it. This sets the stage for future fights and adventures between the people of Kalevala and Pohjola. The story would keep changing because of the Sampo and what happened after it was made. It would change Väinämöinen and Ilmarinen's lives and the places they lived. It wasn't over for Väinämöinen in Pohjola just yet, even though Ilmarinen married Louhi's daughter. The wise hero picked Louhi's youngest daughter as his bride. The Mistress of Pohjola had a hard time giving up her daughter.

Louhi gave Väinämöinen a list of hard things to do. These tests were meant to find out how skilled and trustworthy the person was. The first task was to cut hair with a dull knife. The next thing Väinämöinen had to do was build a boat out of its parts. He was finally told to knot up an egg. Even though Väinämöinen was smart and had skill, these tasks that seemed impossible were hard for him.

As Väinämöinen worked to finish making the boat, he hurt himself with his axe. He asked for help because his magic wasn't working to stop the blood. In Finnish mythology, information is very important. This search for healing turned into a trip in and of itself. During this time, Ilmarinen went back to Pohjola after making the Sampo work. His daughter helped him do the things Louhi told him to do. Ilmarinen married Louhi's daughter because he did well on these tests. This left Väinämöinen without a partner again.

After the Sampo was built, Pohjola had much luck, but the people of Kalevala had a grudge against its strength. Along with Lemminkäinen, Väinämöinen planned to steal the Sampo and use its blessings to help their land. Lemminkäinen is also a hero in the Kalevala. Three brave people got on a big boat and set sail for Pohjola. When they got close, his beautiful song put everyone in Pohjola to sleep. The brave ones got into Louhi's fortress without being seen.

It was held in place by strong roots when they got to the other side. Lemminkäinen tried to get it out, but he couldn't. Because he was strong and smart, Väinämöinen was finally able to set the Sampo free. They quickly added the unique mill to their ship and set sail for Kalevala. Their win didn't last long, however. When a bird chirped, Louhi woke up and knew right away that his things had been taken. To keep the heroes from getting away, she asked for thick fog and strong winds. When that didn't work, Louhi changed into a huge bird and led a huge army of Pohjola soldiers after the ship.

There was a fierce fight at sea. Väinämöinen used his magic to protect himself when Louhi tried to hurt him. It did break into many pieces, though, when it fell off the ship during the chaos. A few pieces washed up on the shore of Kalevala, but most of them went down to the bottom of the ocean. There were a lot of other problems after the Sampo was lost. The parts that made it to Kalevala brought some luck to the land, but not as much as the whole song would have. Pohjola, on the other hand, lost its source of plenty and wealth. This event changed how the two places talked to each other.

He picked up what he could from the shore because he knew that every part of the Sampo was important. He planted these in the ground so that they would grow and bring Kalevala luck. People in Kalevala did this to show how determined they were and how much they hoped for the future.

ANTERO VIPUNEN: WHO STANDS FOR KNOWLEDGE, THE POWER OF WORDS

P eople have told the story of Antero Vipunen for a long time. What the man knows is just as unclear as what he knows about the man. This character stands for old information, lost stories, and a link to the beginning of time. In Finnish mythology, Vipunen is not only very big, but it also holds a lot of magic spells, holy books, and incantations.

Antero Vipunen is important in more ways than one. He is known as a keeper of knowledge. He is a complex mix of the natural and supernatural worlds. He represents the Finnish love of nature and believes in the supernatural forces that run through the land. Vipunen's character shows how deep and complicated Finnish mythology is. He combines parts of shamanic tradition with the epic style of writing that is typical of the Kalevala.

Antero Vipunen is known for being very big, having a strong connection to the earth (often shown as being partly buried or blending in with the landscape), and knowing a huge amount of magical words and spells. Because of these things, he is a scary figure in Finnish mythology, both admired and feared.

As a giant who represents wisdom and old knowledge, Antero Vipunen is a unique figure in Finnish mythology. In contrast to many giants in world myths who are portrayed as cruel or evil, Vipunen is admired for being smart and skilled with magic. He knows a lot about the power of words, the secrets of creation, and powerful spells, all of which are important parts of Finnish mythology.

Finnish people believe that words and songs have power, which is shown by Vipunen's job as an information keeper. People who did this thought that you could control both natural and magical forces if you knew the right words or spells. Since Vipunen knows so much about these strong words, he is the best person to give them to. Many things about Antero Vipunen's personality are similar to magical practices that were common in Finno-Ugric cultures in the past. People used to believe that shamans could move spiritually and enter trances to connect with the spirit world and learn secret things.

Vipunen, being half buried in the ground, can be

seen as a symbol of the shaman's journey to the underworld. Shamans teach their people magic in this way to keep them safe. He can teach you useful things. There is no doubt that Antero Vipunen is a unique character. However, he is linked to other important people in Finnish mythology. He talked to Väinämöinen, the main figure in the Kalevala. That was the most important thing he did. They are connected in a way that shows how Väinämöinen's bravery and Vipunen's quiet but strong knowledge work together in Finnish mythology. Vipunen's personality is similar to that of other characters in Finnish mythology, such as Louhi, the strong queen of the northland Pohjola.

Symbolically, Antero Vipunen is more than just a place to store knowledge. He follows the Finnish belief that spending time in nature can make you wiser. His partially buried state is a metaphor for how real knowledge is hidden and how deep you have to dig to find it.

People have different ideas about what Vipunen is like. Some students think of him as the earth itself, coming to life and holding the secrets of nature. Some people see him as a representation of family wisdom, which is the knowledge that people have gathered over many generations. People today think of Vipunen as a symbol for the subconscious mind or the group unconscious. There are things in this mind that are hidden at first but can be found by thinking about yourself or making art.

The 17th Runo (canto) of the Kalevala is where Antero Vipunen is most famously mentioned in Finnish literature. In the 19th century, Elias Lönnrot put together this epic poem from Karelian and Finnish oral folklore and legend. It is Vipunen who comes to the forefront of the story at a very important point.

Väinämöinen, the hero of this Runo, is making a boat but is missing three magical words that he needs to finish the job. After trying in vain to find these words elsewhere, he is told that Antero Vipunen, who is buried in the ground, is the only being who knows them.

One of the most vivid and remembered parts of the Kalevala is the meeting between Väinämöinen and Antero Vipunen. Väinämöinen goes to where Vipunen is sleeping and, seeing that the giant is still asleep, decides to go into his huge mouth and stomach to make him say the special words.

Inside Vipunen's body, Väinämöinen makes the giant so uncomfortable that he wakes up. Then, there is a fight of wills and words. Vipunen tries to get rid of the intruder using different magical techniques. However, Väinämöinen won't leave until he gets the information he wants.

Several things make this part of the story important to the plot of the Kalevala as a whole. The fact that it does this shows how important magical knowledge is in Finnish folklore. Väinämöinen, who is very smart, has to find Vipunen to get these important words. This shows how deep and complicated the stories are in this system.

Second, the fight between Väinämöinen and Vipunen shows how different kinds of power can clash: Väinämöinen's active bravery and smarts versus Vipunen's passive but huge amount of old knowledge. The fact that this disagreement was solved through sharing information instead of fighting shows the values that are important to Finns when they think about mythology.

From a literary point of view, the Vipunen story is full of poetic images and symbols. There is a colourful description of Vipunen's huge body, which has trees growing on its parts and animals living in its beard. The giant seems like he is a part of the scenery this way.

Antero Vipunen will always have a place in Finnish

culture in the hearts of people who knew and loved him. Artists from Finland, such as Akseli Gallen-Kallela, have drawn scenes from the Vipunen episode that show how scary the mythical giant was and how exciting it was when he met Väinämöinen.

Vipunen changed writing in ways that go beyond just repeating the Kalevala. This figure has affected Finnish writers today. They've used him to show how to dig deep into cultural memory or how to find hidden information. Vipunen has given poets a lot of images and ideas for what they want to say.

Antero Vipunen is back in pop culture in a lot of different ways. Metal bands from Finland are known for using national myths in their music. In their songs and record art, some of these bands have talked about Vipunen. His name is also used for cultural centres and school programs that teach the Finnish language and culture. The character is also used for advertising and tourism.

Today, Antero Vipunen is still seen as an important part of Finnish culture and history. Kids learn about Finnish folklore and the Kalevala through the story of Vipunen in school all the time. The names of many schools and libraries are based on this figure because he is linked to learning and wisdom.

Many artists and writers still change and update the story of Vipunen, and they do it in ways that are up to date. Because Vipunen was linked to the land, people today use him as a symbol for caring about the environment. No matter what area you work in, people are still very interested in Antero Vipunen and are coming up with new ways to understand this mythical person. So far, no one has been able to figure out where the Vipunen story came from or how it has changed over time. The people who study literature look at how each character fits into the story's overall structure and main ideas.

Researchers who study cultures and people have looked at Vipunen in the context of shamanism and the past of Finnish spiritual beliefs. Some psychologists are interested in Vipunen. They see him as a representation of the collective unconscious or the information that can be gained by scrutinizing one's thoughts.

In Finnish folklore, Antero Vipunen only shows up once. However, people from other countries have stories about characters who are like him. Giants who are very strong or very smart show up in many stories around the world. When it comes to Norse mythology, the giant Mimir is known for being very smart and knowledgeable. His job is to watch over the well of knowledge at the base of Yggdrasil.

The Celtic myth says that the huge Bran the Blessed can see into the future. The Titans are figures in Greek mythology, just like Prometheus. Even the gods want to know what they know. These connections show that people are interested in the idea of ancient, often chthonic beings that know everything all the time.

From a psychological point of view, Carl Jung may have called Antero Vipunen the "Wise Old Man" type. People with this archetype know a lot, are wise, and have a strong connection to nature or the spiritual world. Vipunen's partly buried state can be seen as a metaphor for the unconscious mind, which hides facts but can be found by looking for them or thinking about them.

Väinämöinen's trip into Vipunen's body could have been a spiritual quest to learn more or a journey into the unconscious. In many types of tales, the hero goes into the beast's stomach. In Judeo-Christian legend, Jonah and the whale are examples, as are many shamanic initiation stories. A lot of people think that magic words or spells can change the spiritual and nature. The Egyptians believed in heka, and the Hindus believed in mantras, for example. Like many people around the world, Vipunen keeps secret information safe. This is because they have such strong words.

Some interesting things about Antero Vipunen in Finnish folklore are that he stands for knowledge, the power of words, and the connection between people and nature. People are still interested in and inspired by his story in the Kalevala. It also gives researchers a lot to look into. Vipunen brings together old Finnish stories and new forms of culture through her figure. She shows how myths can relate to the lives of people from different times.

TUONETAR: LEGEND OF THE UNDERWORLD QUEEN

People often draw Tuonetar as a beautiful, airy being with long, dark hair and sharp, blue eyes. The fact that she wears beautiful clothes that are both dark and beautiful shows that she is connected to the world of the dead. Even though she plays a scary part, she is also seen as a caring guardian who helps lost souls get to the afterlife. Her appearance is both strong and calm, making everyone who meets her respect her. The Finnish goddess Tuonetar is more than just a death figure.

Her name stands for wisdom and the lessons of life. She must stay in charge in Tuonela, the underworld where the souls of the dead live. A lot of the stories about her are about love, loss, and how life and death happen over and over again. Tuonetar's impact can be seen in many parts of Finnish culture, from traditional ceremonies to modern literature and art. She continues to move and inspire the people of Finland.

The story starts with Aino, a young woman who is very sad about the death of her lover. She becomes determined to find him because she is so sad and thinks he may still be alive in some way. Because she is so determined, she sets out on a dangerous trip to Tuonela, the realm that Tuonetar rules. The River of Tuoni is where Aino's trip starts. It is a dark and dangerous river that separates the living world from the underworld. There are stories that this river is full of whirlpools and strong currents that make it very hard for anyone to cross. Aino is determined, even though there are risks. She gets up the courage to get into a small boat and sail across the river.

As Aino navigates the water, she meets different spirits and animals that live in the river. Some are nice and offer advice, while others are more evil and try to stop her from following her path. Each meeting tries to resolve Aino's issues and helps her learn more about the afterlife. She learns that the trip to Tuonela is more than just a physical one. It doesn't take long for Aino to meet Tuonetar. The goddess appears in front of her and gives off an air of power and wisdom. Tuonetar understands how sad Aino is and how much she loves her lost love. She knows that Aino wants to get back together with him, but she also knows that this will have big effects.

At this point, Tuonetar gives Aino her knowledge by explaining how life and death work. She tells them that every soul has a job to do and that life goes on after death. Aino learns that the person she cared about has found peace in Tuonela. She should stop being sad about him if she wants to remember him well. Aino learns something very important in this lesson: everything is connected, and it's okay to accept other people.

She tells Aino the truth about who she is and how she feels. She finds out that her journey isn't just about finding love; it's also about how tough and strong she is. For Finns, love, loss, and the path of the soul are all very important.

As Tuonetar looks at Aino, she gives her a list of tests to see how much she loves her and wants to do what she says. In the first test, Aino has to find her way through the dangerous woods of Tuonela. Along the way, ghosts and other scary things will try to stop her. Aino needs to show how brave and strong she is as she goes forward with Tuonetar's dim light. Aino has to cross the River of Tuoni again for the second test. This time, though, the currents are stronger. To stay safe in the rough water, Aino needs to be smart and quick on her feet. As she fights the waves, she thinks of all the things she had to give up to get here.

This makes her want to win even more. In the last test, Aino faces the souls of her ancestors, who ask her what she wants and see how determined she is. People say that living things shouldn't be in the land of the dead and that she has messed up nature. They need to see how strong Aino is and how much she has learned from Tuonetar to understand how pure her love is and how important her goal is.

As part of these tests, Aino meets other characters from Finnish stories. These characters either help her or get in the way. When the wise and strong shaman Väinämöinen shows up, he helps and gives Aino advice. He warns her that the trip to the underworld is dangerous and that she needs to know what will happen if she does something bad.

This shows that Finnish society is very deep and complicated by the way Aino talks to these made-up people. From the silly ghost to the wise old man, each figure shows a different side of what it means to be human. Tuonetar is the queen of the dead, so no one dares cross her. Aino can feel her presence when he is having a hard time.

At this point, Aino is not sure what to do after finishing the tests Tuonetar gave her. You have shown him how much you love and trust him. Now, she has to decide if she wants to stay with him in Tuonela or go back to the real world. Because he knows how important it is, Tuonetar tells Aino what will happen if she makes each choice.

While Aino can be with her love again if she stays in Tuonela, she will always be stuck in the underworld. She will never again see the sun or feel its warmth on her skin. Toetar tells Aino that she has to live in darkness forever if she wants to be loved forever. She will always remember her lover, but if she goes back to the world of the living, she will never see him again. Tuonetar tells Aino that the living and the dead are not meant to live together. And to remember the person who died, she needs to learn to let go and enjoy the life she still has.

Though it's hard for her, Aino chooses to go back to the world of the living. She feels bad when she thinks about losing someone she cares about, but she knows that life is a gift that should be cherished. Tuonetar lets Aino begin her climb back to the top.

Going to hell will change her because of what she has seen and done there. Aino learns more about how fragile and beautiful life is before she returns to the world of the living. She now knows that love is stronger than life and death, but it takes sacrifice and acceptance to be real love. Knowing that life and death go around and around is important. The story of Aino shows how strong love can be.

THE GIFTS OF THE MAGICIAN

An old man and his only son lived in a simple hut in a thick Finnish forest. The boy's father, who had lost his wife, loved him very much and wanted to keep him safe from the risks of the world. A group of black-game birds lived in a grove of birch trees close to their house. The boy was very interested in these birds and often begged his father to let him hunt them. Even though the son asked the old man many times, he always said no and wouldn't let them shoot the birds. The father's knowledge and experience led him to make this rule. He knew how fragile nature's balance was and what could happen if you upset it.

They lived in the forest for days on end, and the father taught his son how to get around and how important it is to respect nature. The boy learned how to get food, build a fire, and take care of their simple home. He was still very eager to go looking for the big game. With age, the son became more interested and driven. He wasn't sure at first if his dad's tight rules were important or just a way to keep him safe. He wasn't sure if he should follow the rules or stand up for himself. One day, the dad went into the woods to get firewood, and his son saw a gap.

When he was by himself, he felt the old urge to hunt the black-game birds that had interested him for so long. The boy had to decide what to do. He wanted to do his own thing as well as his dad's. He didn't know that the choice he was making at that very moment would set off a chain of events that would leave him changed for good. Their peaceful life in the forest was about to be turned upside down, taking the young man on a magical journey full of personal growth and surprises.

While his dad was away, the boy gave in to his urge and took out his bow and arrow. As he crept toward the birch wood, he felt a twinge of shame. He pointed and let go of the gun as a black-game bird flew by. But he didn't know much. The bird was still alive when it hit the ground, so the shot did not harm. The boy felt bad about what he did, so he ran to the animal that was hurt and comforted it.

As he got closer to the hurt bird, he changed in a very interesting way. He was shocked when the bird grew bigger and more like a person. Someone dressed as a black game and very strong met the young man. He felt bad looking at the boy, but he was also interested. When he spoke, his words worked like magic. He told them he changed into a bird to test the people who lived in the forest. As he fell to his knees, the young man begged God to forgive him. He felt so bad about himself and scared.

The magician's look changed when he saw that the kid felt awful about what he did. The young man had a chance to make things better. He said he would give him three magical gifts if he could heal his wound. He says these gifts will bring you good things and test who you are. The young man agreed right away because he wanted to make things right and was interested in magic. The witch doctor talked about the three gifts he was going to give: a pretty horse, a zither, and a fiddle while he fixed his wound with magic.

The wizard said that each gift had its special magical powers. The horse wasn't your average mount; it was a smart, loyal friend who could talk. When the zither and fiddle were played, they could charm people and even change what they did. The young man paid close attention as the magician talked. His mind was racing with all the things that these gifts could do. He thought about the fun things he could do, the places he could visit, and the good things he could accomplish with such strong tools.

But the magician warned that there is much duty that comes with being powerful. He taught the young man how to use each gift properly and stressed how important it was to be wise and careful. If the special items are used in the wrong way, bad things could happen. After giving the gifts and giving directions, the magician got ready to leave. Before he left, he told the young man what he had learned from the experience: how important it is to respect nature and how actions can have effects on the world around them that people don't expect.

As the wizard made his way into the forest, the young man stood alone with his new magical things. That was the end of an era in his life. A new part of his trip was about to begin. He was scared and excited at the same time as he got ready for a trip that would teach him a lot and change his life. The magician kept his promise and gave the young man three amazing gifts: a beautiful horse, a zither, and a fiddle. Each of these things had its magical powers that would help the young person a lot on their trip.

The horse wasn't like any other animal. It was tall and proud, and its fur shone. Its eyes were smart. The magic show performer said that this horse could talk and think like a person. It would not only get him from one place to another, but it would also be a smart friend and guide on his journey.

The magician then gave her the zither, a stringed instrument whose sounds are known to calm people down. This zither, on the other hand, had special skills. When played in dangerous situations, it could get help from places you wouldn't expect. Before the young man got into any trouble, the wizard told him to touch the zither.

As the third gift, there was a fiddle, which is another musical instrument with its unique powers. Should the young man's touch on the zither not help, he was to play the fiddle. Hearing its lovely songs could change how people felt and what they thought. This could turn enemies into friends or ease up tense situations.

As an extra safety measure, he gave them a flute. This last instrument was supposed to be used if the zither and fiddle didn't work. The magician stressed how important it was to be careful and follow the rules when using these gifts. The boy paid close attention as the magician showed him how to use each gift. He was told to be careful and smart about how he used them because magical things often had unintended effects if they were misused. The magician told them to be careful with these gifts and only use them when they were sure they would be useful.

The boy got his gifts and learned what to do while being scared and excited at the same time. He had things that made him strong, but they also made him responsible. He could count on the magical horse to be there for him and help him get where he needed to go quickly. After the show, the magician told the boy what he had learned: how important it is to respect nature and how what you do can have effects on the world that you might not expect. He told the young man to help other people and use his new skills for himself.

The wizard said one more thing before he left. People told the young man that these skills were powerful, but they couldn't replace his good character and common sense. How he used them and what he learned from them would show how smart he was. He said, "Thank you very much." He felt thankful and thought of lots of things to do. Before putting the zither, fiddle, and flute away, he made sure they would be safe on the trip. He was happy and scared when he got on his new magic horse.

When the master was upset, the horse spoke to them to make them feel better. The young man thought they could handle anything. As they got ready to leave, the young man took one last look at the forest that had been his home. That was the end of an era in his life. A new part of his trip was about to begin.

There was a small push, and the magical horse took off. It took the young man from the only life he knew to a world of magic, adventure, and finding out who he was. After all, it had learned, the horse knew that the only way to really grow was to try new things and learn about other cultures. Their first stop was a small town close to a forest. The boy met a lot of different kinds of people. Everything was different for each of them. When he didn't have a safe place to live, he saw how hard life was.

The magic horse told him to pay attention and learn something from everyone they met. Everyone they met taught them something. As they went from town to town, the young man felt better about himself. He learned how to get around in markets with lots of people, talk to sellers, and get along with people he didn't know. King sent messengers to meet the young man and made him an offer of huge amounts of gold in return for the horse. The young man had his first big moral choice to make. The money could have helped his family with all of their money problems, but he liked his smart friend and didn't want to give it up.

His magical abilities should take a back seat to ensure the joy and safety of those around him. Some people's lives were spared because of the zither and fiddle. As he and his horse passed through a town decimated by a terrible drought, the young man felt an overwhelming need to play the fiddle. Everywhere he went, people were watching him play. No matter how dire their circumstances, it eased their pain. Most individuals were taken aback when they saw clouds gathering in the sky. A little rain began to fall shortly after that. It felt great when rain fell on dry ground.

As they lauded the young man's lovely singing, onlookers were beaming with delight. They also ended up in the middle of a violent confrontation between two nearby towns on a separate occasion. The young man played the zither to get people to talk and calm down. He did this by using what he had learned on his trips. The peaceful sounds of the instrument seemed to bring people who were fighting together, help them see what they had in common, and end their fight in peace.

These things taught the young man that music could heal, unite, and inspire people. He thought of his skills as more than just magic. He saw them as ways to make the world a better place. It made him feel better about himself, every place he went to, and the problems he helped solve. It also taught him more about the responsibilities that came with his skills. The boy kept thinking about his house and his dad as time went on. He wondered if his dad would be proud of the person he had become after going through many changes. The talking horse knew its rider missed home and told him to teach what he had learned to the people he cared about.

The young man said yes, but he was scared and excited at the same time. The long trip back to the forest hut was where his adventure began. As he went, his mind raced with all the things he had experienced. Someone entirely different had emerged from the naive youth who had disregarded his father in favour of hunting black-game birds. Their approach to the well-known forest sent a flutter through the young man's chest. When he was away from them, he worried about his father. He hoped they could have fun again. The young man started to sob as they reached the simple cabin.

His father was hard at work in the yard when his son sprang up on him from behind. Gratitude and joy welled up in the elderly man's eyes. For a long time, he worried about his son's safety. In the warmth of their hug, the young man started to tell stories of his travels, the incredible gifts he had gotten, and the knowledge he had acquired. Together, they sat by the fire and watched the young man play his beautiful instruments. Songs played in their simple home. The songs talked about faraway places, big problems that were solved, and how strong love and family are. The horse that could talk was glad to see its friend with his dad again.

CONCLUSION

I t's the end of our trip through the wonderful world of Finnish songs and stories. Let's think about all the things we've heard. These stories have taken us to a place where magic and truth mix, where humans and ghosts live together, and where nature's power is absolute. The scary spirit Ajatar, who lives in the Finnish forests, was the start of our journey. The scary thing that it was made us think of how much the Finnish people respected and sometimes feared nature. Folklore uses Ajatar as a warning to show tourists and people who work in the woods that dangerous things are hiding in the trees.

We met Hiisi, the trickster spirit, who was the opposite of Ajatar's evil. The mischievousness of Hiisi made the forest realm more unpredictable, showing us that not all supernatural encounters are simple. The stories of Hiisi teach us to be careful and smart when we go into the unknown because smart people can often beat even the smartest ghosts. Mielikki and her nine boys are an important part of our study of forest spirits. As the kind goddess of the forest, Mielikki stands for the caring side of nature.

Her stories teach us how important it is to treat the forest and its animals with care, and they show that people who are good to nature may get good things in return.

He met us as we crossed over from the world of spirits to the world of gods. He is the divine maker. The stories by Ilmarinen show how much the Finnish value skill and hard work. He is very good at making amazing things, like the famous Sampo. This shows how important new ideas and creativity are in Finnish culture.

Ilmarinen's stories show us that if we work hard and are skilled, we can do anything. Finns have many stories, but the Kullervo story is one of the most moving ones. The sad story of this hero is a stark warning of what happens when you get revenge and how heavy your fate is. Kullervo's journey from a child who was abused to a strong but tormented fighter shows us how complicated people are and how terrible it is when violence keeps happening over and over again.

As we looked around the Swan of Tuonela, our journey became more sad. In Finnish folklore, this beautiful creature that watches over the river of the dead is the thin line between life and death. Swans are beautiful and scary at the same time, and they are often used as psychopomps to help people deal with their fears about death and the future. If we look at the Finns' creation story, we can see how they thought about how the world was made. Finns have a deep connection to nature, and this story about the cosmic egg and the waves of the beginning of time shows how they see the world as having both order and chaos.

In Finnish folklore, Väinämöinen's adventures in Pohjola are a famous example of the hero's journey. As a wise old man and strong wizard, Väinämöinen's quests teach us about sticking with something even when it gets hard and the power of knowledge. During his time with the Pohjola people, the theme of struggle between worlds and the hard things one has to go through to become great comes out. We learned about the Finnish view of the future from Tuonetar, the Queen of the Underworld. Her story is about coming to terms with the fact that she will die and thinking that life goes on after death. The stories of Tuonetar show us that death isn't always the end but a shift to a different state of being.

Last, we talked about the magician's skills and looked at fantasy stories from Finland. People used to think that songs, words, and rituals had power. Finland's beauty is closely linked to learning and being in nature. It shows us that real power comes from understanding and getting along with other people. Several themes and patterns keep showing up in these stories, which give a good picture of what

Finns believe and value. In Finnish folktales, there is always a strong, almost magical link to nature. These stories show a society that got along well with its surroundings. They talk about forest spirits and gods who made things out of natural materials.

A lot of the stories, especially the ones about Väinämöinen and the performers, stress how important it is to be smart and know a lot. In Finnish culture, being able to know everything about the world is often a sign of real power. A lot of the stories are about finding the middle ground between things that are opposites, like life and death, good and bad, and making and destroying. There are two sides to this idea. Hiisi can be both good and bad, and the idea of Tuonela can mean both the end of life and the beginning of a new one. Finns have many big issues, but they are smart and determined, so they figure out how to fix them. What this shows is the Finnish value of "sisu," which means being brave, tough, determined, and able to get back up after going down.

Stories like Ilmarinen's show how much the Finns value innovation and skill. The fact that they thought making things was magical in and of itself shows that they cared about useful skills. Even though these stories take place a long time ago, they are still useful and can teach us important things. These Finnish stories remind us of how important it is to care for and respect nature now that people are more concerned about it. It's important to remember that the earth is alive and should be looked for, not just something that can be used. The story by Kullervo is an example of a complex moral story that makes people think about what they do and how it affects other people. You can use these stories to start a talk about what is right and wrong, what we owe others, and how the choices we make affect them.

The Finns care about these stories and find them important. People like these things because they help them feel connected to their country's past and culture in a world that is becoming more connected. These stories are fun for non-Finns to read because they show how Finns live and see the world.

With their complicated plots and characters, many of these stories show us how people think and feel. They write about fear, hope, desire, and loss in ways that can help people better understand how they feel and what's going on in their own lives. We can think very clearly in a world where real things happen all the time. It teaches us to see things as they really are and not stress over the magic that might be around us through these stories.

It's interesting to think about how Finnish folktales fit into modern life and where they might go in the future now that we've looked at them all. Finns' stories and songs change over time, just like any other living custom. People today write, paint, and make movies that tell these old stories in new ways that are more important to current audiences. It's still about the same types of people and things. People are still interested in Finnish folktales and want to know where they came from, what they mean, and how they apply today.

This study will help people remember and understand these stories for a long time. People work to record and keep these stories living in new ways now that computers are around. Now more than ever, digital archives and internet tools make it easy to find Finnish folklore. This will help it last for many years to come. As more people become interested in other cultures, Finnish folk music is becoming famous all over the world. People who are tired of the usual Western European fairy tales can try these instead because they have a unique mix of magical and everyday things.

The Finnish folktales we've looked at are more than just old stories. You should know this by the end of the book. People still hear and feel those stories today. They teach, amaze, and give them a unique view of the world. Ajatar lives in the dark woods, and Väinämöinen does his magic in the cosmic worlds. These stories take us to different parts of the world. They want us to see the magic in things like nature, the strength in knowledge, and the complexity of life. Remember these stories after you finish this book. Get ready to see the world around you in a new way. Look for magic in everyday things and learn new things in strange places. Folklore can do more than make us laugh. It can change how we see ourselves and the world around us.

GLOSSARY

This dictionary tells you everything you need to know about the most important people, animals, and ideas in Finnish legends and stories. Each entry gives a short explanation of what the word means in Finnish folklore. This shows how difficult and interesting this body of mythology is. In Finnish folklore, there are powerful gods and spirits, magical things, and heroes from the past. Finns have a unique set of traditional values, beliefs about magic, and respect for nature that has shaped their identity for hundreds of years.

Aarnivalkea: Finnish folklore says that the Aarnivalkea is a strange flame that can show you where wealth is hidden. People think it shows up on midsummer nights and leads lucky people to hidden treasure.

Ahti: In Finnish folklore, Ahti is the god of the seas and lakes. He is usually shown as a man with a beard and a trident. As a thank you for safe travels and good catches, fishermen will give gifts to Ahti.

Ainikki: Ainikki is Lemminkainen's sister, and she is known for being loyal and smart. She told her brother when danger was close and helped him on his quests a lot.

Aino: Finnish legend has a tragic figure named Aino. She is known for being beautiful, but she refuses to marry the old wise man Väinämöinen. She drowned herself instead of being pushed into a marriage she didn't want.

Ajatar: Ajatar is a girl demon that lives in the wild. She is often said to have the body of a snake and the head of a woman. People thought that she could give people who met her in the woods sickness and bad luck.

Akka: In Finnish folklore, the word "akka" refers to a group of female spirits or gods. People often connected these ghosts with natural events or certain places.

Antero Vipunen: Antero Vipunen was a giant sage in Finnish legend who was famous for being very smart and magical. Väinämöinen once went into Vipunen's stomach to get special words that would help him build a boat.

Bear: Bears are the most important animals in Finnish folklore, but people often use euphemisms to avoid calling them by their real names. People believed the bear was holy, and after a good bear hunt, they would do a lot of complicated rituals.

Bitch of Pohjola: The scary Bitch of Pohjola stands guard at the gates of Pohjola. People say that its teeth are made of iron and its throat is made of copper. Heros had to beat this beast in order to get to the land of the North.

Etiäinen: For Finns, an etiäinen is a spirit or a nature event that lets them know someone is coming. People thought they could see or hear an etiäinen right before the real person showed up.

Hiisi: In Finnish mythology, the hiisi is a bad spirit or demon that is often linked to holy groves and rock formations. Hiisi could also mean a place of worship or a graveyard.

Haltija: Haltija is a guardian spirit in Finnish folklore that is often linked to certain places or natural traits. The way people treated these spirits affected whether they were good or bad.

Iku-Turso: Finns tell stories about the Iku-Turso. This sea monster is sometimes called a Kraken or a giant octopus. People who were sailors were scared of Iku-Turso because they thought he could make storms and sink ships.

Ilmarinen: An old Finnish smith-god named Ilmarinen was said to be able to make magical things. He is best known for making the Sampo, a magical object that brought its owner wealth.

Ilmatar: In Finnish folklore, Ilmatar is the mother of Väinämöinen and the first goddess of air. It is said that she gave birth to Väinämöinen after floating in the primordial seas for a very long time.

Joukahainen: Joukahainen was a young, cocky bard who dared Väinämöinen to a battle of magic, singing and knowledge. When Joukahainen lost the race, he told Väinämöinen that he would marry his sister Aino.

Kalevala: The Kalevala is Finland's national tale. Elias Lönnrot put it together from stories and myths told by Karelian and Finnish people. The Kalevala was a big part of how Finnish culture and national identity rose and changed over time.

Kalma: Finns think that Kalma is the goddess of things that die and break down. She was connected to the darkness and the death process in some way.

Kantele: A Folk Finnish string instrument called the kantele plays a big role in Finnish myths. The jawbone of a giant pike was said to have been used by Väinämöinen to make the first kantele.

Kave: Kave is a primordial being in Finnish mythology, which is often linked to making the world. Some people say that Kave is the mother of Väinämöinen and other famous heroes.

Kiputyttö: In Finnish folklore, Kiputyttö is the maiden of pain who takes away the pain of sick and hurt people. She was often called upon in spells and practices to heal.

Kokko: In Finnish legends, the Kokko is a huge, mythical eagle. People said that when Kokko beat its wings, it could make strong winds.

Kullervo: In Finnish folklore, Kullervo is a tragic hero who is known for being very strong but also having a terrible life. In the scary and angry ending of the Kalevala story, he kills himself.

Kuutar: Finns call the moon goddess "Kuutar." Some people thought she could send moonbeams and change the moon's phases

Lemminkäinen: Finnish folklore has a story about a hero named Lemminkäinen who is magical, has many loves, and goes on trips. One of the main characters in Kalevala often gets into trouble because he is careless.

Lempo: Lempo is a Finnish word for a bad spirit or demon that is often used as a swear word. Lempo was linked to trouble and disaster.

Loviatar: Some Finnish myths say that Loviatar is the blind daughter of Tuoni, the god of death and the mother of nine sicknesses. In Finnish myth, she was thought to be one of the most evil characters.

Louhi: Louhi was the strong and evil queen of Pohjola in Finnish mythology. Pohjola is the land of the north. She is the main bad guy in the Kalevala, and she often fights against the heroes while watching over the Sampo.

Luonnotar: In Finnish folklore, the Luonnotar are nature spirits that are often linked to the beginning of the world. People thought they were the daughters of nature, and in Finnish myth, they had many roles.

Maan-emo: Maan-emo is the Finnish goddess of the

earth, motherhood, who is in charge of making the land fertile. In agricultural rites and prayers for good harvests, she was often called upon.

Marjatta: In Finnish folklore, Marjatta is a character who gets pregnant after eating a magical lingonberry. Her story is a lot like the Christian birth story, and it shows how Christianity came to Finland.

Mielikki: In Finnish folklore, Mielikki is the goddess of the forest and Tapio's wife. Hunters often called on her for good luck and lots of games.

Nyyrikki: In Finnish legend, Nyyrikki is the god of hunting. He is often shown as the son of Tapio and Mielikki. Before going on a journey, hunters would make gifts to Nyyrikki.

Otso: In Finnish tradition, otso is one of many polite words for bear. It was thought that using these names would show respect and keep the strong animal spirit from getting angry.

Päivätär: It is said that Päivätär, the Finnish goddess of the sun, makes the sun move across the sky every day. People often prayed to her for good weather and lots of food.

Pekko: The Finnish god of crops, especially barley, is called Pekko. He was linked to having children and making beer.

Pellervoinen: In Finnish folklore, Pellervoinen was an old god of plants and trees who was linked to their growth. In agricultural practices and prayers for good harvests, he was often called upon.

Pihlajatar: In Finnish folklore, Pihlajatar is the spirit of the rowan tree and is thought to have protective powers. Bark from rowan trees was used in spells and rituals to keep away evil spirits.

Piru: Piru is a Finnish word for demons or bad spirits in general. Piru could refer to a number of different bad spirits that caused trouble and bad luck.

Pohjola: Pohjola is a magical northern land in Finnish folklore that is often portrayed as a scary and dark place. In a lot of the stories in the Kalevala, the characters go to Pohjola and fight the people who live there.

Rauni: When it comes to Finnish folklore, Rauni is the wife of Ukko, the thunder god. She was linked to the rowan tree and to being fertile.

Sampo: In Finnish folklore, a Sampo was a magical object that brought wealth and luck to its owner. A big part of the Kalevala's story is how the Sampo was made and then stolen.

Saunatonttu: In Finnish tradition, the saunatonttu is a house spirit that lives in the sauna. It was common to leave gifts for the saunatonttu to make sure they had good steam and a good time in the sauna.

Surma: The personification of violent death in Finnish folklore is called Surma. People often thought of Surma as a scary monster that killed its victims quickly and cruelly.

Syöjätär: In Finnish legend, a syöjätär is a bad witch or ogress who is known for eating people. She was often shown as a danger to kids and tourists who weren't careful.

Tapio: In Finnish folklore, Tapio is the god of the forest. He is usually shown as a respectable man with a beard. People who hunted and worked in the woods would give Tapio gifts to bring them luck and safety in the forest.

Tellervo: In Finnish folklore, Tellervo is the daughter of Tapio and Mielikki and is linked to the forest. Hunters and people looking for food in the forest often called on her.

Tonttu: In Finnish folklore, a tonttu is a house ghost that looks like a gnome or a brownie. Tontu were thought to keep the home safe and bring good luck if they were treated well.

Tuonetar: Tuonetar is the Finnish goddess of the earth. She is often shown as Tuoni's wife. Together with her husband, she ruled over the land of the dead.

Tuoni: The Finnish god of the earth and death is called Tuoni. In his world, Tuonela, the souls of the dead lived.

Turisas: Turisas was an old Finnish war god who was sometimes confused with the Norse god Tyr. People called on him to win battles and keep them safe during times of war.

Ukko: In Finnish folklore, Ukko is the most important god of the sky, weather, and thunder. In Finland, he was one of the most important gods, and people often prayed to him for good weather and plenty of food.

Vellamo: The Finnish goddess Vellamo is the wife

of Ahti and the goddess of water. She was linked to lakes, rivers, and the sea, and fishermen often called on her to help them catch big fish.

Väinämöinen: Väinämöinen is the main hero and wise man in Finnish folklore. He is known for being wise, singing magically, and going on many adventures. He is one of the main characters in the Kalevala and is often thought of as the classic Finnish hero.

Vetehinen: The vetehinen is a Finnish water spirit that is often described as being able to change into either a person or an animal. People who lived near lakes and rivers were afraid of vetehinen because they were known to trick people into getting into the water.

Virankannos: Virankannos was a Finnish folk tradition in which a bride was taken to her new home by boat. People thought that this would keep water ghosts away from the bride and make sure that the marriage would be happy.

Vipunen: In Finnish folklore, Vipunen is a giant sage who is famous for knowing a lot about magic spells. Väinämöinen had to go into Vipunen's stomach once to get special words that helped him build a boat.

Ylermi: Ylermi is a small Finnish god who is linked to death and the future. People thought that Ylermi led dead souls to the underworld.

Made in the USA
Monee, IL
24 November 2024

71104593R00069